BLOODMERCY

WINNERS OF THE AMERICAN POETRY REVIEW/
HONICKMAN FIRST BOOK PRIZE

1998   Joshua Beckman, *Things Are Happening*

1999   Dana Levin, *In the Surgical Theatre*

2000   Anne Marie Macari, *Ivory Cradle*

2001   Ed Pavlic, *Paraph of Bone & Other Kinds of Blue*

2002   Kathleen Ossip, *The Search Engine*

2003   James McCorkle, *Evidences*

2004   Kevin Ducey, *Rhinoceros*

2005   Geoff Bouvier, *Living Room*

2006   David Roderick, *Blue Colonial*

2007   Gregory Pardlo, *Totem*

2008   Matthew Dickman, *All-American Poem*

2009   Laura McKee, *Uttermost Paradise Place*

2010   Melissa Stein, *Rough Honey*

2011   Nathaniel Perry, *Nine Acres*

2012   Tomás Q. Morín, *A Larger Country*

2013   Maria Hummel, *House & Fire*

2014   Katherine Bode-Lang, *The Reformation*

2015   Alicia Jo Rabins, *Divinity School*

2016   Heather Tone, *Likenesses*

2017   Tyree Daye, *River Hymns*

2018   Jacob Saenz, *Throwing the Crown*

2019   Taneum Bambrick, *Vantage*

2020   Chessy Normile, *Great Exodus, Great Wall, Great Party*

2021   Natasha Rao, *Latitude*

2022   Chelsea Harlan, *Bright Shade*

2023   Jane Huffman, *Public Abstract*

2024   Jacob Eigen, *The Twenty-First Century*

Bloodmercy

I.S. Jones

The American Poetry Review
Philadelphia

Book design and composition: Gopa & Ted2, Inc.
Distribution by Copper Canyon Press/Consortium

Library of Congress Control Number: 2025939069

979-8-9875852-3-8 Bloodmercy paperback
979-8-9875852-4-5 Bloodmercy hardcover (limited edition)

FIRST EDITION

The American Poetry Review
1906 Rittenhouse Square
Philadelphia, PA 19103

www.aprweb.org

CONTENTS

Introduction 1

After the Offering Ritual, Cain Carries Abel Home 5

❦

Cain 7

Hands of the Field 8

Juice or Milk 9

Sister's Keeper 10

Vanity 12

Just the Four of Us 14

Daddy's Girl 15

Patience in the Bramble 16

Cain in the Peopleless Kingdom 18

Contempt Towards Eden 19

Bloodmercy 20

We Are Soft Between Hours 21

❦

Abel 25

Epithalamion in the Field 26

A Brief History of the World According to Goats 27

Feast 28

Psalm of Acquiescence 30

Between Grace and Mercy 32

First Sighting 33

Nocturne 34

Kitchen Work 35

Twice as Many Stars as Usual 36

❦

First Drought   39

Sister's Dress   40

Psalm for the Fast Girls   41

Fawn   42

But Never the Same Love Twice   44

Field Notes in the Final Days of Girlhood   45

Mark of Cain   48

Husbandchild: Etymology of Cain   49

Psalm of the Morning Twerk   50

It's Vast Enough to Pretend   51

David   52

Self-Portrait as the Blk Girl Becoming the Beast
Everyone Thought She Was   53

A Lot of Blood but Not Much Mercy   55

The Terrible Feast of Love: Etymology of Abel   56

To Will It   58

Of   60

Eve   63

Eve onto Lilith   65

Angel's Trumpet   67

Land of Nod as Nigeria   68

Bloodmercy   71

Acknowledgments, Notes, & Gratitude   75

INTRODUCTION

I.S. Jones' long-awaited debut collection, *Bloodmercy*, asks, from its opening to closing poems: *What does mercy look like?* Rather than fully formed renderings, Jones offers composite sketches—images mined from the poet's sharp and singular vision. With verse from the perspective of Eve and a thread of poems reimagining Cain and Abel as sisters, *Bloodmercy* wrestles with the idea of grace vis-à-vis myth and memory, gender and sexuality, with the utmost urgency. The seriousness with which Jones treats both subject and craft is as impressive as it is inspiring.

In twelve convincing lines, "Contempt Towards Eden," for example, considers the "uncountable years" Eve spent in the Garden. More prison than paradise, Eden's sublimity bores the hell out of Eve. So, too, does the power dynamic between herself and Adam, that "strange creature named husband" who, we learn, brutalizes her, "dragging [her] by the throat." Eve admits to having double-crossed God for her own amusement. This betrayal, typically thought of as man's fall, is, *Bloodmercy* makes clear, the earliest instance of female insurgence and empowerment. By the poem's end, Eve reminds Adam of her agency, while promising to expose his abuse.

> ...*One day, I will tell our daughters*
> *every time you touched me it was a violence*

Similar to "Contempt Towards Eve," "Patience in the Bramble" takes place in a time of supposed innocence. The speaker recalls a childhood game played with teams of boys and girls, the hunters and the hunted, respectively. Having shot her first kill at eleven, the speaker's huntress qualifications fall on deaf ears. When she subdues one of the hunters with a knee to his jaw, the boy's mother calls her an *animal* for resisting the ruling principle of the game: boys on one side, girls on the other. The speaker agrees, concedes that she is "just a fawn trying to escape the bullet's appetite."

With an eye towards intersectionality, "Self-Portrait of the Blk Girl Becoming the Beast Everyone Thought She Was" further challenges and complicates gender expectations. The poem begins with the moon, the object of legends that, by its fullness, turns man into beast. Surrounded by wolves, the speaker interrupts her own animal transformation, reflects: "born non-white & woman," phrasing lifted from Lucille Clifton's "won't you celebrate with me," a poem honoring Black women's resistance and resilience.

Any hint of animalism, the Blk Girl knows, evidences her imagined savagery. Though she has, to date, been gracious, "a snatched tongue: polite hands: crossed legs: a settled throat: plea & please," the Blk Girl prays to god to be consumed by passion. She pleads:

> ...teach me to lose my mouth in reverie
> to laugh in my predator's blood   to let it fill my belly

The Blk Girl, I believe, also desires a witness to this consumption. A witness who will attest to her humanity—someone with whom she can express the full range of human emotion, including rage, without fear of dehumanization. Range is one of *Bloodmercy's* many strengths. Subtlety is another.

How fitting that Jones christened the collection *Bloodmercy*, as mercy so often follows blood. To the extent that even the title bleeds into the first line, the poem "Between Grace and Mercy" makes much of blood, "the body's first covenant," as the speaker describes. The bleeding title, this small gesture, demonstrates Jones' flair for world-building. A dog is skewered by a fence's rusty rails. A hare's entrails ornament asphalt. The poem is utterly distinct, yet completely in dialogue with the work surrounding it.

In "Husbandchild: Etymology of Cain," the speaker reveals the meaning of her name: "she who creates; crafts; forms." Whether or not this revelation is autobiographical, I.S. Jones has certainly created, crafted, and formed something breathtaking with *Bloodmercy*. Jones takes on the idea of grace, at whose feet we kneel and at whose side we wish to heel, and does so with lyric intensity and precision. Since I am feeling particularly blasphemous, I reckon that somewhere a religious text is missing a psalm. Find it here in *Bloodmercy*.

Nicole Sealey
January 29, 2025

BLOODMERCY

†

AFTER THE OFFERING RITUAL,
CAIN CARRIES ABEL HOME

Violence is a failure of communication.
The shoulder severed from the dream of the socket.
Most pain is useless
but it's the body's oldest song.
I want my own suffering to be intimate.
I do what I can to ease Abel's wailing.
The goat's final gesture to dethrone
her from the stone altar, to stir its might
against its master. The beast saw the light
but not the blade. Abel saw the resistance
but not the panic. I had never seen so much blood
moan from an animal's throat. To unburden
the beast of its crimson gown, which dresses
now my sister's sutana. Heaven's blue flame
laps the goat up. Despite our best labor,
eventually Baba comes to collect. It's either the animals
or us; the best of the harvest or the soil
will consume our true names. We have blood and dirt,
together they make God. And what does mercy look like
between humans? A sister reaching to lift a sister
from the ground. When I say a love that will end us,
I mean 'mercy.' Remember, I offered you my hand once.
Push me away if you like.

"[...] We have high time for work and another meeting
women exchanging blood
in the innermost rooms of moment
we must taste of each other's fruit
at least once
before we shall both be slain." —Audre Lorde, "Meet"

"It does not, therefore, depend on human desire
or effort, but on God's mercy." —Romans 9:16

CAIN

Only Abel saw headless goats in the swirling eddies
      the summer we were grown enough to ride
our bikes past the stop sign. Truth is I trust my memory
      more than I should: two sisters having separate girlhoods
to say they survived. We had so much fun before
      we understood the rules. I tell this to the bat-eared fox
with its hindquarters in the maw of another animal,
      its left orbital bone, crushed. Reprieved by no shade,
no vegetation, safe for the husk of tree hollowed out from rot.
      I look to the fox, its throat shredded into red whimsy
and say aloud, *I too can be cruel sometimes.* Above, a red dress torn
      and snagged on its branches. So, this is grief:
stillness before devastation. They never found her alive—
      the girl Abel was with that day. Vulpine creature, I bare no
salvation for you to consume. If mercy is a decisive blade,
      then let me deliver you. Just as I did Abel in a dream,
where I say, *Let's go out into the field, sister.* Her: in a nightgown
      surrendering to the wind's grasp —
cool nightfall gutted us with moonlight. I say *Follow*
      and she does because I say my hands will bring her closer
to Baba's glory. We walk into the open mouth of dusk.
      Her: holding my hand & I almost felt my humanity
from the well inside me come back up where I push
      it down; she trusts me to be her shepherd—
to lead her beside still waters. When I felt the misericorde
      give way, the neck bone doubles under my tending,
it felt good to know a taste of God's might.
      Call me merciless lover. Sister. Equalizer.
She who plucks weeds before they threatened the harvest.
      She who isn't afraid of her gluttonous hands.

HANDS OF THE FIELD

To teach me anything, Mommy says, *Watch my hand.*
Soon, I learn to braid my hair by repeating her wrists.

Same hands slapping lotion on our faces each morning,
she taught me *the sun rises in the East, sets in the West*

so, I'm never lost coming home. Sight, a pattern of witness,
I learn to hand-sew, to count in Roman numerals,

How to avoid the living room when Adam begins his subjugation.
First, mumbling. Then, screaming. His fists penetrating her skull.

As we do during a thunderstorm, we hide under the covers.
"Sometimes" by Britney Spears croons from each earbud,

and we sing to each other to close the distance. What little I understand
of marriage is better understood in my garden. Sumac in the spring,

poison oak sprouts their green worlds in shade. Symbiosis requires peace
or obedience. Abel returns home each evening with fresh lamb, skirt steak.

I, sweet peppers, yam, spinach. Adam gets the lion's share of our labor
and for another night, our mother can rest. Cups of water collecting under
   our bed.

JUICE OR MILK

I was born angel-tongued, though no one knows it now
Mommy spoke Yorùbá, and I spoke it back to her

If we always talked in the language of angels, we were always in prayer

And so, when teachers gave each child a snack during lunchtime,
they asked, *Juice or milk?* and I repeated back the sound,

not understanding a tongue so flat, so rote

In isolation, language dies on the tongue. I covet my little Yorùbá,
keep sparse these words like silver dollars, remembering:

Mimo [meaning 'holy', meaning 'clean']. Ife me [my love]; omi [water];

Iyọ [salt]; Bimo [soup]. Diẹ iyọ, meaning *More salt*
evokes "ischemic" and "hemorrhagic." Keeping close:

Gba [take]; Fi mi silẹ [leave me alone]; Ọdẹ [meaning "dumb"]

Ode [meaning "hunting"]. I was a child but smart
enough to know a father's curse.

Smaller men need power just as God needs people to forgive.

SISTER'S KEEPER

For years, I have loved you in the dark—
your heart pulsing in my throat as I waited

your arrival, weary traveler.
Mama told me very soon I wouldn't be alone.

Long enough to tell the dark's madness from my own,
each night, I peeled back my skin to unveil a body

Baba would find use in. I was born to watch over you
& you were born to keep my hands purposeful.

Mama said you are mine.
Mine.
Mine to hold & hold

beneath me. You were born
to give what I could not,

so you came into the world
the way miracles do:

                a swelling   eyes shut

        rupture—
           then

a dragging into the light. When you grew
to meet me in the eye,

I don't remember how it happened:
your little skull was split

open, & this was the first time
Baba heard your blood

moan. You wailed like a salted
prayer—   wide & endless—

& I think I cried too,
my small face wet & quivering.

Mama called us into her presence
told us to bite deep into

each other's flesh. I watched you
kiss flowers into mama's hands.

I opened my own mouth & oleanders
bloom with the vision of hunger.

VANITY

It's summer & all day we did what girls do:
spoil our appetite with sweet bread we steal

& hide in the folds of our dresses.
We are picking the lock on our mother's bedroom

to dive for treasure. We take what we want:
gold earrings   rouge   red lipstick

her sewing needles & nail lacquer.
Mommy calls for us to do chores, but we run

laughing headlong into the new world
governed by cicadas.

You reach for my hand & we become one erratic body:
two-headed, four-legged, barefoot galloping

toward the emerald field. We feast on a banquet
& I paint your nails (blush for you; dark green for myself).

When you finish eating, I ask if you're ready,
trap you between my legs,

remove from its wrapping a sewing needle,
pull taut the waxy flesh of your earlobe.

Breathe for me, I say & you do.
Then the needle punctures flesh.

I open you & we stay this way for a while: your hands
squeezing my thigh, earlobe's crimson drip.

Again, you say & I pierce the other,
wipe you on my dress. Ruby stars your ears now carry.

Before the trek back home, we bury
the lipstick & rouge & nail lacquer in a cedar box.

I never washed your blood off my dress,
the vermillion wave that every night I hold

close to my nose & inhale.

JUST THE FOUR OF US

In our beginning, there was so much we didn't need—
fences, bulwark, caution, curfews. Dense and deciduous,
the firs made us equal to the creatures calling it shelter.
Baba opens His eye to the new day & much of the labor is complete.

Sister follows the herd dog to round the cattle, and I pick the garden
of plums, grapes, strawberries so that Mommy can press each
into a final sweetness that I soon will covet in mouthfuls. Sacred
is the process of rot. Back then, I laid in the cellar for so long

I could hear the wine age. Noble to the senses, I know each person
in the house by scent, by sound. Frankincense, amber, lavender, mint.
I remember perennials this way: sumacs, garlicky, for spring. Bee balm,
deer resistant. Hyacinths heady of spring. At day's end, Abel takes my hand

and we run through the night's gossamer. Foxtail grass kiss our ankles.
Nothing else alive on earth but us the animals cloaked inside. Night being
a different kind of nakedness. There, on the other side of the river,
was darkness touching darkness, light gathering in a thin cluster

like a great eye opening. I was nine and unafraid; I didn't know
I needed to be.

DADDY'S GIRL

Lord forgive me, I am my father's child: ·
cunning and arrogant with beauty.
Adam's first. Daughterprince.
No one beneath God tells me what to do.
Sly and nimble, I'm called "mischief"
more than my own name and so when I caught
Adam smoking he rewards me with love.
Him with my obedience. My girlness is bound
beneath overalls to Momma's disappointment.
What she couldn't corral beneath a dress or brush
back into even barrettes, she sent to Adam.
We exchange glances, laugh with our eyes.
She doesn't get it and how could she? I am 8
and can only see my mother for her gender—
exhausted to a numb, wounded, bitter
to the touch. The feminine urge to be
my father's best boi, I boy'd better
the other boys—peed standing up,
won every game of 'nut check,' shot
my first kill by 10, caught trout by their mouths
at 12, could spit a perfect parabola in the air.
Boylaughed at the other girls for their softness.
Feral against the demure, I am handsome
for the boymouth that refuses mercy. Lot's wife
is a common story; a tale told from mothers
to daughters about disobedience. Shame measured in salt.
When the first blood came for me—
my girlness was treated like of a fox. Deceitful.
Adam stopped hugging me, yes, but the other boys
rejected me from the tribe. O Father, I have been a girl
all my life. I have no other history. No other master but You.

"What kind of girl are you? The kind who wants to live [...]'"
—Vievee Francis

PATIENCE IN THE BRAMBLE

I don't remember squeezing the trigger,
though I never forgot the smell of gun smoke.
Of the wild dog's eyes ruined between rage
and confusion. How I waited too long to shoot
and the beast an eyelash short of my throat
when the bullet pierced its chest.
I don't remember Adam handing me the misericorde
but the blade never forgets completion.
Blood darkening a halo about the animal's head.
There were many animals slain beneath me.
Then other girls. I never started the fight,
but I always ended it, and sometime the fighting
ended me. On my back. On my knees. Loose braids
from another girl as trophy. Again, Momma hollering
I've torn another good frock. That I refuse to behave
like a proper girl. More rough than gorgeous,
because my girlhood is fox-shaped. Knows how to hunt
and how to be hunted. Instead of 'I love you,' Adam
teaches me how to curl my hands tight, how best to stand
for balance. All these years, I thought he was trying to bond,
I understand now it was to inure me to danger, so that when
boys came, I knew their movements before they did.
Obedience only afforded me an enemy's failure. The boys
thought they cornered me, but what I lacked in height,
I made up in precision, so I pulled the tallest one
down by the collar and kneed him in the jaw.
I wanted the boy to learn what life had yet to teach,
that's what I told his mother when she called me an 'animal.'

An animal on her haunches who must now outrun
the riot of boys. Imagining the years of running laid bare.
I can shed my velvet but not my girlhood.
A girlhood mothered by scraps, fathered by a fist.

CAIN IN THE PEOPLELESS KINGDOM

Can one be opulently tired? If so, I am here:
dress pockets spilling of acorns, allegro in half shadows
praying mantis scaling the length of my forearm,
scraped knees: the signs of a good childhood well spent.
A ladybug lands on rotting fruit that when I split
between my hands, an encore of maggots spills out.

All things in the lush world have their place. Any field
is a church once you understand surrender. I wear
my sister's blouse with my mother's skirt. I am 10
and if I was faithful to patience, the fields beyond
my tending opened their secrets.
Show me a creature more resilient than faith—wildflowers.

Every winter, they retreat forming beneath the earth,
a whisper of revenge. And every spring, they resurrect.
I make bouquets & speak to my subjects: *I dreamed you once.*
Did you feel it? Daisies in their proclamation: *Yes. I am*
your dream made root & flesh. Red clover, white clover,
red clover, white clover, make me in your image.

Cornflower. Lady's glove. Meadowsweet.
Because I think I'm so clever, I'll tell you something:
I think some of us were born to give more love
than what we will know in return. And that is killing some of us.
Like what Adam does to my mother, dragging her
by the throat into the bedroom.

CONTEMPT TOWARDS EDEN

Milton gets the tale about me wrong: Paradise is boring.
I ate of God's Golden Heart[1] and betrayed heaven for myself.
In the uncountable years of the Garden,
I lived wild and never cooked. Ate only of the earth's freshness.
I was born motherless, and mother/less is the wound
of my motherhood. My kingdom of remorse. My father in Heaven,
there is no evenness in your world, only this man dragging me by the throat.
Only this strange creature named "husband" sinking his rage
into my stomach. The word "shame" did not reign me
until my eyes flung against light—cutting open my cornea,
brown yolk spilling out. One day, I will tell our daughters
every time you touched me it was a violence.

1. The hapus mango, for its heart shape and sweetness is referred to as "God's Golden Heart,"
which is also the forbidden fruit of the Garden of Eden

BLOODMERCY

Summer begins its descent & we waste the hours in love
with our girlhood: red popsicles drip on our good dresses,
our legs carry us through the wild grass, skin sighing against
each green blade, your hand scratched on bark,
me finally mastering the two-strand twists I practice on you
because your hair finally grew past your shoulders.
It's us two under the low hanging expanse. *Your hair is so long,
I'm jealous,* I whisper. Say to wisdom, *You are my sister,*
& call understanding my kinswoman. I wanted to deliver you
from cruelty & gave you my own instead. Beneath your long skirt,
a tapestry of rubies. I rinse your legs with the backyard spigot.
My life made sense when we were of one mind & two bodies.
Now, you keep secrets from me. Your diary says as much.
The seasons turn & we stop knowing each other. *Take my hand,* I say,
& we tangle ourselves in the hammock. When your head lulls
onto my chest, I notice your hand is still bleeding. I pull a bobby
pin from my hair, bend it straight, open my skin. My blood meeting
yours to become "cainabel." My name eating yours to become
"cannibal." Mercy at your still body becomes "claimable."
Call it "grace" or "pity," you my ancestor, my wife, I should
have ended you when the stakes were lower. Wound of my wound,
immutable bond, my heart unknowable from yours becomes "chainable."
Clarity arrives as patient light: No matter what wind will drive us apart,
you'll never leave me.

WE ARE SOFT BETWEEN HOURS

There's a sweetness to these nights of surrender.
It's true, the heart beats two rhythms: one for me, then you.

I emerge from the shower, drip on Momma's good floor,
trail a gown of water towards your door.

Down the hall, you stretch in your skin, I saunter in mine.
I tried before to rest but my jaw aches from grinding teeth,

so, I kneel at your altar. I watch you touch yourself
through a blade of light leaking into the hallway.

Earlier, we went to the river if only to relieve
the body of the sun's tirade. I didn't mean to see at first:

you slip out of your blue bathing suit, step into the water. Blue promise
memorizing the muscles of your back. I'm old enough to understand

too much longing can make any creature feral. My problem
is that I fall in love with beauty. You are the grape going into my mouth,

the lone tear of riverwater tracing my breast. I've spent my small life
as two bodies yearning to be one. I want to know how it felt

the first time you discovered God's eye blooming between your legs.
A flowering of dark red poppies in a field. What pleasure possesses you,

sister, I want for myself. In this night, everything is about the moon—
even her absence, even you. Eventually, someone wants something,

that's the nature of power. O patient light, grant me passage. I want
no beast but the night to hear me. Your soft, indelible labor,

fingers roving the field until you shutter into a gilded song. I long to kiss
the hands of this submission. I dream we crash into each other:

cainabel cainabel cainabel. That even when you catch me
& close the door, I fever for the taste of you. I said I have a problem

I didn't say I wanted to be saved.

✝

ABEL

Baba gave me dominion over all cloven & two-legged animals.
I lift my hands & all living creatures bow.
I stir shadows & creatures plunge headfirst to salvation.
Some of us pick flowers, dream in blue & green,
others do the real work to bring home a heavy feast.
All year long, my people eat like kings.
Look at me, Cain: Baba's most prized creation.
He made life, but I undress the light
& a village doesn't go hungry
of the way I put my humanity on a nightstand
to do the vain, hideous things,
what sister, do you know about blood & the way it speaks?
I remember each upon each—the knuckling, the wordless pleas,
the clean deliverance of blade upon a beast's neck.
Flesh into flesh.
Every nation under my tending feasts until marrow
until tendon
until muscle
until blood is savior over body.
Let each column of teeth
know its guillotine weight.
Let each hungry mouth know itself to be a brief church.
O sister, praise me for the pity I have shown you
& know when life gives you poverty be grateful life gives you
anything at all.

"And when I go towards you it is with my whole life"—Rainer Maria Rilke

EPITHALAMION IN THE FIELD

As a deer longs for streams of water, so my heart longs for You,
how the red, wet animal in my chest throbs Your name.

I gather a garland of the day's eye, sew a crown of branch and nettle,
bleach clean the antlers of a fallow.

Before ceremony, the church pews sing a language of hunger.
Every beast I've slain has come to bear witness,

fill each seat with their mangled bodies. I'm so close to madness,
Father, stretch my hands, guide me towards Your light.

You who knows and whose vast knowing undoes me—
the rush of my blood is You.

The faithful pacing of my lungs is You.
Forfeit my eyes in lace, and I'll still feel You.

Come find me, Baba, in the church of wheat and sunlight.
Before You, I am disciple, bride, guardian of Your perfect name.

My body is merely a tool of execution. Take me as yours
and I will follow You. O, how possible I feel in Your light.

A BRIEF HISTORY OF THE WORLD
ACCORDING TO GOATS

In the Fertile Crescent, goats domesticated humans to learn goat tongue
        but now are domesticated for slaughter

Goats dream in the equivalent of seven human hours & by this estimation
        goats will render technological advances obsolete in 10,000 years

Goats count human days in lashes, counts years by the rings around the eye

Between the rise and fall of empires, goats domesticated humans to follow herds
        as a symbiotic form of life

Shifting from an agrarian culture to an industrial one contributes to goats
outpacing humans

Damascus goats are deformed because they ate of God's Golden Heart

It's been said when you eat a goat's eye you dream of its life

The hock has cured ailments, pastern for anguish, flank for love

A normal presentation of a kid birth signals a plentiful harvest

Famine has been preceded by an abnormal herd

A kid born polycephalic will be abandoned by its mother

Goats are born with panoramic vision to see death

Goats plan for war as does any animal

This is a poem about rot

FEAST

I confess: Dawn is my favorite animal
because it is the only one I cannot kill.
How its cobalt fur gallops off Baba's shoulders,
charges across the thin-black horizon
in hooves of gold and grapefruit
to cleave the day open. Every morning,
I feed the chickens, give hay to the goats,
milk the cows, and on and on.
Baba told me to bring home veal for supper.
I would be lying if I said I wanted to do this.
There is no pleasure in it for me.
I've never liked the taste of flesh anyways.
Hunger is a savage god all bodies must kneel to
and it's hard to desire anything you've made submit.
The trick to slaughter is leading the dumb beast
to a false deliverance.
The beast must be kept calm, fear spoils good meat.
Once, mommy swung a chicken over her head,
its neck pulled taut to breaking.
What besides love inspires such pain and cruelty?
Then, she made me kill a scared lamb
and its meat made everyone sick.
Yet every season they eat and eat
convinced, I think, it somehow makes them better animals
than ones they consume.
But why protest when it's just so easy to live this way:
my forehead knelt to Baba's feet.
I'm disgusting anyways.
Me: a plague made flesh.
I destroy so what lives may continue its destruction.
As Baba commands, I command the animal to follow
and it obeys.

I lead it behind the barn and it obeys.
I stroke its fur, lay its neck down the same stump.
I produce a machete.
Its eyes meet my eyes.
I pull its neck towards the sun.
It knows what I know but does not beg.

PSALM OF ACQUIESCENCE

¹Not the neck's calligraphy
or the blade's singular desire
to divide spirit from flesh,
but Baba,

²bless this animal
for offering up its blood
and delivering a bounty
of satisfaction,

³for granting the hands of the shepherd
her greatest ability to baptize
a nation, ⁴to keep bellies full
until hunger comes to my altar
again

⁵*Make me to hear joy and gladness that the bones*

I have broken may rejoice. May the soil open
its merciful jaw to consume the beast's bones
as it will consume me one day.

⁶*Behold: I was shaped in iniquity and in sin*
did my mother conceive me.
⁷Baba, let me rest as this beast rests:
eyes glazed looking for a heaven
cruel enough to say 'open.'

⁸*Deliver me from bloodguiltiness,*
O Baba, God my salvation
and my tongue will sing aloud of your righteousness.
⁹As I bring down the blade again
let this beast's teeth

hooves

        horn

  tail

          tongue

flesh—ignorant flesh—be a reprieve
from death. [10]Either I am
a murder or the field between
grace and mercy.

[11]Let every beast
know its purpose, to lay its neck
upon a slab of surrender.

[12]Let every blade I wield become a fang

of light. May the world be simple
and kneel at my command. Amen.

BETWEEN GRACE AND MERCY

we learned mercy so young: a beetle with its hind legs crushed.
a dog impaled by a rusty fence. a hare thinking it was clever enough
to reach the other side of the road. a veil of light drapes each moment—
red, tangerine, azure, lavender, each waiting to reimagine the sky.
the beetle frantic to undo what sudden brute force divided its from legs
still moving towards a song. with the beetle, it was simple.
Cain crushed the small creature with the heel of her foot, splayed open like
    a wish.
people think suffering is meant to be purposeful, otherwise why name it.
maybe i am nostalgic for what wounds best. the hare & tire & the asphalt.
the asphalt gowned in viscera makes a new animal. a dog leaps too low &
yelps all evening for Baba into the orange-pink sky.
all day blood weeps into the rust. rust twisted deep into the animal.
i take the dog's face in my hands. touch is the body's first language.
blood is the body's first covenant. *kill it*, says a sister.
you kill animals all the time. i kiss the dog's eyes closed.

FIRST SIGHTING

"Girl-born" but not a girl, not a boy: a beauty in the space
between experience and celestial. they touch me, and I come
into new knowledge: infinity bound into flesh. There are parts
of the future I reject—like despair. More than this evening,
or a bountiful harvest, what I desire most in long evening
stretching itself out—is you. Before its completion, I knew
the day was perfect. The course of my life widening after eating
a pretty boy's pussy. No longer am I ashamed to want.

NOCTURNE

It comes to me when I struggle:
your hands learn a kind of mercy about my neck,
how blood rushes to the center of departure.
When I had to kill a lamb this way,
Cain called it lovework—
the ritual of hands tightened against faith.
Above the surface of flesh,
I thrash against Mommy's cool touch
returning again to that dark grasp.
It comes to me when I struggle:
not Cain but something she did to me
that only blood has language for.
What will Time do this body
that she hasn't already named?
Let me present myself plain, Old Master:
In the dream, I walk for miles in a dark forest.
I wouldn't have known my own face if daylight
handed it back to me.
A soft hand snakes about my throat
& it's my sister's face I meet on other side of betrayal.
Some animals show mercy by devouring their lovers.
O Lord, honeyed by fireflies, blood drips from your chin
& I know it is my own.
Making real the dream of my suffering,
the sun drags its headless body across the sky like a monument
of war.

KITCHEN WORK

I used to believe it was a conjuring: three clicks—
fire and its seven tongues lapping from the stovetop,
bubbles rise from the metal floor and begin its rhythmic churning.
Mommy says to cook, you must bring together everything you love:
olive oil   onion   garlic   tomatoes   basil   sprig of thyme
The tongue can tell what is fresh from what is left petrified in the fridge.
I grind fresh habaneros and the labor pickles my eyes red.
Maybe I'm not the flower bearer, but I am a romantic. Once I opened my heart
and now I cut my garlic fresh. Outside this kitchen,
my hands are an omen, red blade, legacy of moral surrender.
But here my hands are alchemical: fish flank in the pan, I say *I love you,*
I need you to survive with my hands and no one goes hungry in my house.
Mommy teaches me how clean a fish: In the neck's opening
pull out the fish's red accordion, open its hull with a blade,
unburden the fish of its organs like some macabre celebration.
Red sky in the afternoon, red sky stirring in my pot, I make my stew slow.
Each of us knows a recipe for poison. I know my sister is allergic to peanut oil.
I consider the red accordion in her throat: her hands clawing, as any animal
     would,
for air. I consider the alchemy of the oil churning through her body,
the invader moving like shadows in her blood. Her blood revolting
into the color of winter. I put my dreams back in the cupboard.
I cut my sister a bowl of blood oranges, her mouth gleaming
a warning in the light.

"But tonight, he is alive and in the north field with his mother."— *Laura Gilpin*

TWICE AS MANY STARS AS USUAL

Here, in a night so black I close my eyes and become the night itself.

For the arduous winter ahead, I braid down my hair. Trim my nails short. Fold
away
my summer frocks. No time for beauty when there are mouths to feed. In my
backpack,

a mother's tools: feeding bottles, space heater, ruffage, a spoonful of cunning.
To get to the future, I shed my old self. Wrenched you, my child, bloodbent &
defiant to life.

Still fragile about the ankles, Ife staggers towards me when I open the barn door.
For a goat's mother left its only kid to die of neglect, I offer up my heat

in absence of the other animals too scared to come close.
Now, I'm your momma. You are as perfect as any child I could have birthed
myself.

For what, if not love, could bring me to my knees in this hay and cold?
Instead, you need me so, I am with you. Baba, you painted every star

and know each by name. Sometimes I am selfish enough to pray,
"May I go before you so I will never know another night outside your eyes."

Forgive me all the times I took your life for granted. Tonight,
you are alive and recovering, though devastated to your knees by a shooting star.

The sight itself reminds us wonder needs a witness. I pull cobwebs
from the grapevines and eat.

†

FIRST DROUGHT

Before expulsion,
I could see a sliver
of the world beyond
my garden. Now,
Eden is a brain blink
between migraines.
I didn't understand "drought"
until the angels left me.
Husband is gone west
while the land exhausts
from overuse. It would
be alright if he never
returns. Ideal, even.
A confession
I slip into my eldest's
ear, one where
her eyes answer back.
My oldest says I triangulate,
my youngest says
I'm never on her side.
They're both wrong.
To stop the fighting,
Abel moved into her own
room. One bit the other,
I don't remember which.
Called Abel by her sister's
name for a week before she
corrected me. Still, the person
I take care of most is not
even myself. I will look back
on our suffering worn into stone:
Father, if you can see me, weep.

SISTER'S DRESS

Abel often says I like to take things that aren't mine—
Like the boy's book I stole because he was mean to me.

Or the time I lifted your toothbrush
because I wanted to know the mouthfeel of you.

Sister, follow the singular thread between
intimacy & urgency & you'll find me there. Yes,

I stole your socks & stockings. Your bluest frock
blotted scarlet. Your ruby studs & clumps of hair

left in your comb. So desperate I was to know you at all,
I stole your diary in the absence of your tenderness.

Covet you in pieces to make a sister who would love me.
Lay the stained dress next to your empty side of the bed to sleep.

"Desire prefers the hunt to the kill"— Contrapoints

PSALM FOR THE FAST GIRLS

[1]Girls like me are born armored against "cunt," against "hoe," "whore" too. [2]"Slut" is just a dagger of a word, how it slicks my tongue to laughter. To break my enemy's neck. [3]My breasts, ruddy nubbins, arrived before I knew the words "sex," "bend," "suck." [4]Call me a "bitch" if you're brave enough to collar me. [5]It took too long to know what boys meant by "DSLs". My lips already a fast girl's red. [6]Thirteen & my legs are "too sexy to be seen." [7]Baba, boundaries of danger & awakening have fallen for me in pleasant places; surely I have a delightful inheritance. [8]Born beneath the banner of Eve's transgression, [9]I learned from other girls to leave home in packs. [10]Slip a razor blade under the tongue. Misericorde under my pillow in case boys come to hunt me in sleep. [11]Not a girl to them, just myth. [12]A story traded between other boys as proof of prowess. [13]Much of the hunt is homoerotic—men pleasuring men through me. [14]I do catch them on the walk home massaging my legs with their eyes; the walk to school & slow-moving cars behind me; [15]the crosswalk guard smiling too long; boys using flip phones under my desk if my legs were spread wide enough. [16]Nudes saved & the rumors of nudes never deleted. [17]& like my mother, I'm bored of the expected positions. Nothing about them is edible, not even their desires. [18]Baba, I won't spend my days on my back as useless meat. [19]One day, I went looking to be the trouble. [20]Wore one outfit at home, switched clothes once outside. My eyes a charming offensive each. [21]Where I'm from you get called "fast" for looking boys in the eyes for too long. [22]Just as arrogant as the bat-eared fox who puts her head in the wolves' mouths, I am as dangerous as rumors say.

FAWN

for Belinda, with gratitude to D'Angelo

he only hit me   because i didn't get out   of the way fast enough each palm formed

       against a child   is meant to wound them   into understanding

    instead of heirlooms   my mother passes down her shame

    pulls taut my hair   says *it's disgraceful to be a girl*

who likes to please   in the gossiping circle   a girl flashes a hickey on her wrist

      rhododendrons in heat   her badge of budding sexuality   shame
         touched me

before anything else could reach my father stopped   hugging me
when the first blood came

      i could wash myself   but was never clean   enough

i never touched anything   but when i did it was for slaughter   to earn my keep

      in the tribe of girls   i let a boy give me a hickey   to endure it

i dream my first girlkiss —   lips   soft of   rosemary & lavender

      mother calls out   my sister's name   & i don't correct her

i could labor my way to beauty   to love   mother lies to me   & i say *thank you* mother says no one will love me if i'm fat & i starve myself to husk

she leaves the room every time i cry & suddenly,   i am cured of all feeling

    dishes after dinner are left   for me to clean   & i say *it is my pleasure*
      to please

so desperate to be a creature someone wanted i possess a new face

    to mask   who i am   i'm not myself when alone   not myself

around others   i am disappeared   in all the temples   i have made   of people

    shrine of disgrace   before this altar   i cover my bare scalp   kneel my
      head

to the god   i've made   in the image   of my mother's approval don't worry

    i promise to live up to your disappointment

BUT NEVER THE SAME LOVE TWICE

the boy who would rape me once touched me softly
between the breasts, tracing each scythe impression—
two moons cresting into dark. telling me to be careful
of wearing bras too tight.
the entire weight of his body against me: soothing. here,
with my shirt to chin, i trust him, complete as an omen,
as though his touch alone could undo the first wound
of femininity. i tell this story now to momma instead
when she asks me for his name. when other girls asked,
they whet their cruelty across my face—whore, cunt, bitch.
i need a mother, not the wrathful arrow of God. is my life
worth, at least, the gentleness to spare

FIELD NOTES IN THE FINAL DAYS OF GIRLHOOD

In high school, when someone asked the teacher about the length of a summary,
     He replies, *Think of it like a woman's skirt:*
      long enough to cover the subject but short enough
      to keep things interesting

To spell together, a male teacher drags the word out: *to-get-her*

The male roach locks its leg around the female, penetrates with its stinger.
     all the boys around me laugh watching the female struggle
      they chase & pin me down my father finds us right as one boy
     mounts me   shoots at them   blames me for being so loose

The lovers in mutual surprise

A priest chases us girls from the dilapidated church,
slacks to his ankles, the woman's sweetness still on his face

I learned: secrets are the currency of girlhood

Adam once used my computer to watch p*rn
     which I only know because he left the discs
     in my laptop

Curious about the sound of creation,
     I replayed the discs under my sheets

When the priest lifted his head from the woman's legs
his face was satiated, saturated to splendor

I too eager to taste the source of such delight

my mother tells me I'm around girls too much
>   I dream my small world a mirror— soft red soft dress
>   soft curls attracting the soft morning dew

In *500 Days of Summer*, Summer sits at her vanity as a child while the
    narrator explains,
Since the disintegration of her parents' marriage, she only loved
two things: the first was her long dark hair, the second was how she could
cut it off & feel nothing.

Momma shaved my head for refusing to have it in braids

A synonym for 'aberration' is 'mirror,' a synonym for 'mirror' is 'sister'

My sister is beautiful, I am useful

When my sister asked why I shaved my head,
>   I told her it felt good to destroy
>   something of me she loved

when I stopped desiring you, I found myself
>   to be more beautiful.
>   I couldn't remove my lips
>   from my reflection

To be a girl who drinks from another girl's mouth
>   not on a dare

Now my thighs darken at every kiss

But how to tell my mother I was never a virgin. Already,
>   I've tasted the sweetness of a lover. Already their
>   head burrowed in my bus & rose up full of my honey

Each time I arrive closer to confession, Momma reminds me
    We live in an ever-changing world made by unchanging god
    & for a moment I felt embarrassed to have witnessed her pain

plagued by the knowledge that her daughter is gay
    she tells me, if you love me, you will give up
    this lifestyle

In Toni Morrison's *Sula*, I learn grief is a floor
    that can eventually be touched

Just like the dog thrashing itself on the other side of the shared wall

Sister called it "another loud dog night"

Growing up, the term "Lot's wife" meant
"a woman who refuses the wisdom of God"

At winter's encroachment, we've lost four hours of sunlight

Darkness swallowing the landscape behind us

As children, we once believed we could outrun
night if only we heeded our mother's voice

Now, like a woman who never learns, I look back

MARK OF CAIN

First, a voice called my name
from the deep loom of my legs,
a soft ache of the interior
which grew many eyes and switchblades of claw.
What dam in me that kept the beast in the dark—
opened.
The voice renamed me
into a red fulfillment
and I knew I was unable to stay a girl.
The blood came onto me the way a flood
looks down on a village.
Such primordial knowledge
stained all my dresses.
Baba said this is my gift instead of death:
The Mark of Cain.
That every month my gift would return
with a pain more dazzling than the last.
Said He did this because He loved me
despite my wicked heart:
Suffer in My name and salvation will reach you.
I understood what I was becoming:
bestial before His immaculate eye.
Unclean in holy spaces. Unable to touch my sutana
unless a man sanctified me.
Carnation heads cleaved from their stems.
You claim to be a god of mercy, but hear me:
My God, you have no idea how well I see You in the dark.

HUSBANDCHILD: ETYMOLOGY OF CAIN

The first return of spring I could remember,
Momma took me out to the landscape,
said, *Burrow your hands into the soil & listen.*
So, I did. I am daughter & husband. Sister & mother.

My name means "she who creates; crafts; forms."
The world I wanted most was one that would bend
at will. I didn't understand this as a child,
when my first Narcissus wilted in the heat.

It was the law of my home: Because I'm older,
my sister does as I tell her. She cuts me a bowl
of blood oranges and I delight the spoils. Firstborn.
Third parent. Mother of my own haunting lack.

Was I allowed my youth or was I just a surrogate to salvage
my parents' union? I keep my nails short and my heart planted
in the ground. My hands have come to know the wet dark intimately.
My parents only touch at night, plea each other's name.

Sister calls me "Perverse," and I say "How?"
Frogs envelope their softness into each other.
Wild horses mount their mates to undo
an ancient appetite. The soil tells me as much.

In my tantrums, I cursed the Narcissus, it said *Yes lord*
then perished at my feet. I know what love is
because I know what violence is capable of.
Truth is: I have no husband habits.

Mother weeps in my lap with her good eye unblackened by Adam's rage.
Baba, You have given me this dominion to master.
You want perfection, yet You want the labor done
by human hands. How do I win if there's no pleasing You?

(Cain)

PSALM OF THE MORNING TWERK

[1]Bless these knees & the tendons keeping the knees
in place that I bounce morning light from cheek
to cheek. [2]Make heavy the clap of my thighs
worthy of its own nectar, [3]knowing that love
and loneliness are mantras nourishing this form.
[4]To be reaffirmed in the body's holiness,
I put my hands on my knees & look back at it.
[5]I forgive myself any embarrassment of the flesh,
[6]spirit above my own dignity, I surrender to delicious
desire of myself. [7]For feeling is a form of knowledge.
[8]That I may outlove my shame. [9]That you could scatter
my love across a barren field of spring.

IT'S VAST ENOUGH TO PRETEND

If pinned between desire and awe, then i am just as good as any witness to the water trailing down the lush curve of your back. your arms. your hair just barely past your ears. It's late summer and you emerge from lake michigan a prayer long traveled from the lips of the eager to the hands of the hopeful. hands hopeful enough to grab my ass & i say "thank you." say "for symmetry, you must grab the other cheek least it be left lonely." the lake begins its climb back to shore. looking out, it's vast enough to pretend we could be anywhere: costa rica, mumbai, here with the singular bee saved from a watery descent. you asked me to leave with you & the answer is "yes," but that's not the lesson. we could fold a small life into four months, but that's not the lesson either. towing the frightened bee to shore, i learn new language for trust. how to love someone open knowing how it could end. but there is no ending with us, just how to begin & how to begin again. braids slick back, it's easier to dive beneath the crest. you feed me a slice of fruit & say "i like when you do gender fuckery." i like how you boyblush for me. your love was the first lesson, your leaving the other

DAVID

I loved you when I was a child
and so, my love for you was childish.
For nine lifetimes, you've haunted my dreams.

Nine lifetimes of finding me in the tender hours
that hang low enough to touch.
Which doesn't help ease me to sleep.

You marked in memory: lips—overwrought
of sweetness, mouth like a too worn,
kicked-in fence. Green eyes pursuing me

through the years. So quiet your lashes against my breast,
I could mistake you for faith. Zora says it's useless
to justify desire, and so, dawn betrays me to sunlight.

I say I have no use for nostalgia and still, you return,
not as the man you are now but as the boy, I loved at 16, at 17.
Knowing nothing of love then, I understood devotion

but not who was worthy of it. All my life,
so much of the grace I gave at the cost of grace for myself.
We could have wasted the hours in a heady field of spring,

called it a marriage. Maybe all childish love is the fleeting light
I will never touch again. In the dark, I bite you with my softest teeth.

SELF-PORTRAIT OF THE BLK GIRL
BECOMING THE BEAST EVERYONE THOUGHT SHE WAS

the moon is my first emotion   then beast   then happy rage
depending on a zealous appetite

i pull bobby pins   from the kitchen of my scalp   tear out nails

one by one   pluck out the lashes   yank docile teeth

        fold the skin back by the mouth   i release my human flesh &
          night drops

blue wolves circle the block in acute madness
dreaming in gun smoke & new names to pick their fangs clean

          the moon sways blood & voices behind yellow eyes,
          each of the names bow inside me.

i grin   & the moon is an anxious pulse   i, a hungry one

      in overexposure, the moon could make anything feral
i only eat a macabre light & the night is so sweet on my tongue

      fear makes the blue wolves multiply

the moon rummages through the light of my name like a vagrant beggar
    tills the blood in my four-legged body

      born non-white & woman, call the thing what it is:

hostile   uppity   neck-rolls   hips without the logic   mean-mugs
    vengeful at the root

but you've only known   my mercy

a snatched tongue: polite hands: crossed legs: a settled throat: plea & please
    two hands on the same body

    never my unhinged joy

in my first language—the cease of blood before writhing—

knuckling of bone & sinew   a blue neck caught inside a maw

& how each muscle negotiates   before severing

god of the faithful night,   teach me to lose my mouth in reverie

    to laugh in my predator's blood   to let it fill my belly

how it trickles   through the floorboard of my teeth

A LOT OF BLOOD BUT NOT MUCH MERCY

It never feels as good as the first time:
the ruddy scab giving way to a persistent fingernail
until bright pink flesh beneath opens.
Blood weeps out then plasma.
Mouthwatering satisfaction.
And I know it's disgusting—peeling myself like this.
In my brief mania, I seek cleanliness by renewal.
My lips scab & I couldn't leave those scabs alone either.
Susurrating sewing needles under new flesh, Baba,
I could take apart your machinery and make myself
red and pink and aching in each corner. I pick, and Adam
catches me in the rearview mirror.
It's the most attention he offers up in a season.
Tendering the flesh made inevitable pains congruent.
But I know it was an accident when my mother wrenched
the front door over my foot and my father near-split
my finger with the car trunk latch. Though I knelt towards
silence, like I was trained to do.

THE TERRIBLE FEAST OF LOVE: ETYMOLOGY OF ABEL

I.
Here's a truth about the world and the people who live in it:
no one wants to touch the dead body, yet everyone waits
to consume its flesh. It's a story I know now by heart:
a girl goes into the forest and returns a woman against her will.
Her dress torn. Hands anointed in blood. Soil and tears veil her face.
In this house, war solves only one problem: the desire to wage war.
Surrendering to the body's feral instructions, my family carves up
my pet goat, Ife. Ife, Yorùbá, meaning "love." Imagine that:
eating love. My family eating my Love. They sit upright
at the dinner table, clinking silverware, Love filling their mouths.

II.
The line between *beast* and *human* is a fallacy of conquest.
It's all the same war: animals devouring animals.
Maybe I should be grateful it's not me at the table's center—
on all fours stuffed with sweet peppers, garlic, and sage.
My name, noble as the wind, and like the wind, I am invisible.
They delight in my labor and not a single "thank you."
Ife and I were the same: creatures no one wants.

III.
Adam's one silver tooth tears into the meat of Love.
When he sees I refuse food, we stare at each other.
We carry two narratives. In one, he is a good father
teaching me my place in the world. To beat me into softness
as if to say *I'll teach you to love me.* In another, he walks
with the arrogance of a king but no wealth. Give people freedom
and they invent better cruelties. Give a girlchild an axe
and she comes to understand beheadings can be pleasure too.

IV.
I am the axe dreaming my way through Adam's throat.
The blade and neck have a long relationship of lust. Some mornings,
I would sit on the bathtub's lip watching Adam shave his neck,
silver trowel over the dark earth. The axe is only a weapon
when knowledge fully forms. My name meaning "threshold,"
"ephemeral," "vainglory." I am the space between resistance
and flight. The axe drags its one fang across the sun's face
before diving back to earth. One beast becomes two. No one knows
I can't wound a creature without turning the knife on myself.

TO WILL IT

No one fears being born, but my sister did
Baba said *Birth a child in pairs so neither one*
              will be alone
      sister never noticed her birthday pictures
      were actually of me
Fragile, you came into the world,
still your birth brought home war
Nights Mommy reached for the remote, Adam grabbed her
       by the neck, rammed her head through drywall
Starved himself to spite our mother,
       he would only eat
       if she served his food
       on her knees
Before her birth, Abel knew what kind of man our father was—
desperate for power, we knelt to him by fear. Until tonight,
when I pulled you to safety, despite your wailing,
As though my sister was embarrassed to be alive,
       she never got over her colic
Rubbed dirt into a new dress Mommy made her wear
Had her head shaved
for refusing to wash her hair
In spring, the strawberries I grow were never sweet
     to her liking & she threw them into slaw
     for the chickens & goats to make feast of
So unhappy my sister, she'd be miserable in heaven
Saw her soul reflected in a deformed goat—only creature
       to love her without judgment. Had I ended you, sister,
        when the stakes were lower, maybe now we wouldn't be galloping
       into the threatening forest
Yet I couldn't tighten my grip enough
around your throat enough to will it

First love: moved away   Her goat-son: dead
Weeping tulips, her head in my lap   Wailing made her useless with grief
        The past hemorrhaging our mother's wails, the future:
        dark corridors collapsing us into fable—
tender, into the woods, we go—

OF

Of Celestial
Of porous faith
Of spite
Of the lick back
Creature made of
    tendons & rage
Of the pious eye
A bankrupt vision
of heaven
Sister of the discarded
Daughter of the rose thorn
    piercing a footpad
Daughter of ash
Of second-hand exile
Sister of the shared
    toothbrush
My side of the bed
'Help' is an admission
    of need
Need is a doubling of desire
Of my blood
Vulgar scent of slaughter
Daughter of my father's shadow
Out of love to give
Of mercy's fang
Daughter of
    the first sin
Of my mother
    and her lack
    of mother before her

†

EVE

I know Death
is the undulating snake below the Great Tree.
Before Truth opened my eyes
I could do nothing but feel—
even the veil that blocked my sight
could never make me ignorant of desire.
I knew of my nakedness—
the snake's tongue throbbing
for the meat of my thighs.
I am a feral thing; my mouth
a greedy canvas of ripened consequence.
In the garden, I pick fruit & masturbate—
worship myself in the absence of prayer.
The blackberry's sweet nectar indistinguishable
from my own.
Fingers: blackened   Pussy: blackened
Lips the color of shadows.
All day, I dance like a rich woman
let mango drip from my chin.
You don't know hunger, a throat relieved of its own drought,
until your teeth tear open the wet heart of the sun
& chew through its shining meat.
I don't know if I could have broken the snake's spell–
or rather if I wanted to.
I followed it—sliding & sliding—
through the quiet bend
where stood God's second head.
I pulled God's heart down from the branches.
I sunk my teeth through salvation &
climaxed like never before.
I wept & then all the lights of heaven focused through my skull
like a dagger's epiphany.

I woke up naked & wailing in a forest;
the faint caw of life at midday,
flies rest lazily on leaves
as shelter from the coming rain.
I know Death:
it met me at the edge of myself
gave me a new name,
then sent me back.

EVE ONTO LILITH

When he touches me, it is you I feel, sister.

When I catch my reflection in the river, I see your face.
Gold-winged warblers open the morning with their trill & I know it is your
laugh.

When the winds lifts my dress, just so, I know it is your breath.
I spend my days looking for you. Your blood sings to me from everywhere.

I ask Adam if he had a lover before me & he calls me hysterical—
slaps me so hard, blood & then more blood

fills my mouth, ruptures in my eye. I wail & hit him back. He breaks
heaven over my skull & the world goes dark. Sister, it goes on like this.

At night, he fucks me so hard, I bleed. He moans *repent repent repent* until he
comes.
He won't look at me now, says my greedy mouth is the collapse of paradise.

Some animals show mercy by taming the wild out of their lovers. I laugh at
his rage,
I laugh at my loneliness. In the agreement of flesh, he keeps me small. I keep
him purposeful

God tells us once the miracle comes, we have to leave Eden.
He doesn't explain what 'miracle' means,

but says 'punishment' means 'deliverance.' Sister, I'm scared.
I don't understand what's growing inside me.

Days uncount themselves. My body, gorged & overripe.
God tells me this is my gift instead of death.

That I would create life the only way a human can.
I've never flinched before a man & I don't intend to start now.

Your body is a spell I summon from dust:
Lilith, deliver me.

ANGEL'S TRUMPET

And when I sunk my teeth into God's Golden Heart,
    I fell to the bottom of Creation,
      then I heard.
A song existing out of time & space.
The way the sound entered me,
    I could taste its coppery ring.
ascending between earth & darkness,
the whole of humanity galloping
      through me.
No human can carry the weight of Your knowing.
The horn forcing its way from my skull
    is called "migraine"
Lord, You make sure punishments
are as exact as your mercies
Each time the pain greeted me, I couldn't stop
my life from tumbling forward.
      Again, something as whole as salvation
      opens—
That sound. My belly swelling over ankles
    bloating in the heat.
When I could take no more, there You were
blistering with perfection.
      Pendulous horns called on my sister,
Lilith, when, at last, her crowing skull—
    Turned me to mother.
The pain of childbirth astonishing,
    all I could do was focus
    on the cellar spider
    hiding in the Angel's Trumpet.
When I woke, I gave birth to my own mother.

LAND OF NOD AS NIGERIA

In the beginning, we carried our faith & practices
from the First World to the new & so we called
ourselves "Celestians," each follower a lit match
of the Holy Spirit. When it comes to us,
Baba, we are pinned beneath need and fear. Love,
as you call it. It is in heaven as it is with us, Celestians.
What does death mean in paradise? Once, I returned
to Nigeria and nearly died of liver failure. Once, I
govern a kingdom on a leash. Lord, the home I was
loved is gone. I tell this to my daughters when they ask,
Where is your Nigeria? Not death, but the symbolism
behind slaughter. Wandering land. Valley slumbers
East. For the faithful left home to give their offspring
a future unmoored by loss.

†

BLOODMERCY

Now that one sister is seven years returned, so too is the other.
          Into Cain's eyes, the oleanders suddenly loosen their sutanas &
                    sweep heady perfume about our ankles.
A mirroring of faces creased into separate womanhoods.
I once thought it reflexive— how I reached for you
                    like another limb fixed into place.
Our gestures circling the other—your long fingers,
          my scalp racked clean of worry;
                    my upturned wrist; your lips press
to the skin; I trip & you twist your ankle;
loneliness clouds your mind; the pain invades my dreams;
                    I bite the blood orange; the juice colors your mouth.
Speak your name into Baba's ear & you stand before me.
As promised in youth, memory returns us to dig
          for that cedar box buried in the woods. It's true, sister:
time elongates its reach
                    & soon your childhood fits into a palm.
The future bisecting the past. On this lone hill where heaven stops
just short of our shoulders. You were more than my sister:
                              you, my child,
guardian, ancestor, my husband & wife: I do
carry you with me all my days & even when the maggots
          will make tender work of our flesh.
I close my eyes to see you with my heart; I close my heart
          to see you with The Spirit.
What we knew to be 'love,' was more habit than conviction.
          To live, I remove the yoke bearing 'sister'
& leave you here. Nostalgia & origin are two points
                              that come to meet again,
the singular braid forever binding our fates—
                    fox to hare; myth to song; mercy to sister.

†

ACKNOWLEDGMENTS, NOTES, & GRATITUDE

Immense gratitude to the editors and publications in which, sometimes, earlier versions of the following poems have appeared or are forthcoming:

580 Split— "Angels Trumpets"
Agbowó— "Daddy's Girl"
The Auburn Avenue— "Between Grace and Mercy," "Compline"
The Brooklyn Rail— "Bloodmercy," "Husbandchild: Etymology of Cain"
Blood Orange Review— "Vanity"
The Chicago Reader – "Contempt Towards Eden"
Granta—"A Brief History of the World According to Goats" and "Cain"
Guernica— "Epithalamion in the Field," "After the Offering Ritual, Cain Carries Abel Home"
Hayden's Ferry Review— "Mark of Cain"
Honey Literary— "Kitchen Work"
Luna Luna Magazine— "Eve," "Abel"
Nat.Brut—"Sister's Keeper"
Prairie Schooner— "Cain in the Peopleless Kingdom"
Poetry Column NND – "David"
Scalawag Magazine— "Patience in the Bramble"
Shade Literary Arts— "Psalm of Acquiescence"
Southern Indiana Review— "We Are Soft Between Hours," "The Terrible Feast of Love: Etymology of Abel"
The Rumpus— "Nocturne"
Transition Magazine— "Eve onto Lilith"

✝

"Vanity" was selected as a finalist for the 2020 *Blood Orange Review* contest.

"Cain In the Peopleless Kingdom" is after and owes gratitude to Mary Oliver.

"Patience in the Bramble" owes gratitude to Vievee Francis.

"Hands of the Field" comes from Vievee Francis's poem "Taking It": "A woman like me with soft hands not hands of the field, but hands meant to stroke and soothe needs a weapon [...]."

The opening line to "Epithalamion in the Field" is Psalm 42:1. "Psalm of Acquiescence" uses lines Psalm 51.

"Psalm for the Fast Girls" uses line Psalm 16:6.

The version of "Between Grace & Mercy" that exists in this book was re-published in *Poetry Onl*.

In collaboration with the poet and visual artist Gabrielle Bates, "Epithalamion in the Field" was republished as a poetry comic in *Poetry Northwest*.

"Nocturne" uses lines from Audre Lorde and Octavia Butler. "Juice or Milk" and "Land of Nod as Nigeria" are for my mother.

✝

I give thanks to The Most High, for He is good. For His mercy endures forever.

I owe a bouquet gratitude to some of my teachers over the years, whose unwavering devotion and care established my foundation as a writer: Romaine Washington, who made sophomore high school English class not only a lush exploration of literature but brought poetry to me and changed the course of my life. To have reconnected with you late, as an adult, has been such an incredible gift. Thank you for everything, Romaine. It's an honor to make you proud. Everyone who buys *Bloodmercy*, say "Thank you, Ms. Washington!"

Dr. Leilani Hall, the living great woman that you are. You saw greatness in me before I had the courage to see it for myself. You took me in your hands and sharpened me. Your *Theory of Poetics* class changed everything I understood about my craft. Thank you for clearing the path ahead. Thank you for believing in me.

My thesis advisors, Sean Bishop and Amaud Jamal Johnson: Honestly, the thesis committee of my dreams. Thank you both for pushing me and making me surer of myself. For giving me the space to dream so audaciously.

Immense gratitude to the following institutions whose resources made this completion of this book possible: Hedgebrook, Callaloo, Brooklyn Poets, Wisconsin Institute for Creative Writing, The Watering Hole, Bread Loaf Writers Conference, & I owe a special thanks to The Black Arts Consortium at Northwestern University.

I owe endless bouquets of gratitude to my rockstar, hero, marvel, Elizabeth Scanlon, who went above and beyond to make my debut one for the history books. Thank you for being *Bloodmercy*'s midwife.

To my great loves that I trust with my life:

Julian, without your siblinghood, care, and friendship, there may not have been a *Bloodmercy* at all. That day in 2017 when you called me before I boarded my train may have changed the course of my life forever. You were the first homie in the squad who got their book picked up, and I learned so much from you as I have over all these years of being shaped by your love. It's the honor of my life to know you, to love you, to be loved by you. For over 10 years of friendship, you have been there every step of the way. Honored to write alongside you, beloved.

Nicholas, my sib. My first chosen family. One of the great loves of my life. It is your friendship that healed my heart in a way I could write into and through the complexities of the ideals *Bloodmercy* is negotiating. The moment I saw you, I knew I wanted you to be in my life forever. Thank you for choosing me back. Thank you for the love you poured into me. Thank you for keeping me alive, wild, bright, and endlessly possible.

Zora, how eager I was for true sisterhood before I met you. My favorite editor, the Pimp C to my Bun B, my soju drinking buddy, what an honor it is to be loved by you. A love that alights my life with color and shape. To be in your light is like being seen twice. For the hours we poured over these poems, for the exacting questions you asked of me (not only with these poems but in life), I am a better person in the world having met you. So much of what I learned about a healthy sisterhood, I learned from you. For the years behind us and the years to come, I'm so lucky I get to roam through this life alongside you. I could have lived 1,000 lives and never have known a love like this.

Gabriel, my love of loves. Somehow, despite the years, we were able to hold on to each other. I give thanks. I give thanks for how we grow up with each other. We grew each other. There are very few people I could say are my day ones and you are that. You held my hand until the 11th hour of turning in the final draft. You hopped on the phone, talked about line edits, and held me every step of the way. As you have the whole of our friendship. You remind me how I come into the world fully made. It's the honor of my life seeing the person you have grown into. I love you so, so, so much.

For friends, beloveds, heroes, colleagues, I owe each of you a bouquet of gratitude: Gabrielle Bates, Sarah Ghazal Ali, Kwame Opuku-Duku, Karisma Price, Henneh Kwaku Kyereh, Kweku Abimbola, Saba Keramati, Stuti Sharma, Patrycja Humienik, Kim Young, Precious Okpechi, Tamilore Osho, Camonghne Felix, Faisal Mohyuddin, Daniel B. Summerhill, Noel Quinones, Ebenezer Agu, Jari Bradley, Miller Oberman, Loic Ekinga, Séamus Fey, Kay E. Bancroft, Saddiq Dzukogi, Carly Joy Miller, Jada Renee, Brittany Rogers, Ajanae Dawkins, Vincente Perez, KB Brookins, Jade Yeung, DeeSoul Carson, Kameryn Austin Carter, Rob Colgate, Hua Xi, Vivian Hu, Lindsay Kelsey-Garbutt, Adrian Matejka, Dorothy Chan, & to Belinda Munyeza (Though we are no longer in each other's lives, thank you for the time we were sisters. I wish you healing. I wish you happiness). And to every colleague whose path have crossed mine, I thank you.

And to Baarish: Thank you for the love of a lifetime.

www.ingramcontent.com/pod-product-compliance
Lightning Source LLC
Chambersburg PA
CBHW030854090426
42737CB00009B/1221